THE NATURAL WAY

Roma Havers is a queer poet, theatre-maker and unsolicited go-go dancer – from your hometown but living in Manchester with their partner, allotment and every stone they've ever pocketed. Commissioned by Orchestra's Live, Manchester City of Literature and Manchester Museum, among many others, they are known for their 'joyful, communal and tender' work. Alongside their poetry work, they have produced writer development programmes, mentored many poets and produced work for performance including their show *LOB*, which toured the north-west and Belfast in 2022, with their play Helmet with Laughter Lines being longlisted for the Bruntwood Playwriting prize the same year. They were winner of the 2024 Northern Writers' Award for Poetry with *The Natural Way*, their first collection with Carcanet.

ROMA HAVERS

THE NATURAL WAY

POEMS

CARCANET

First published in Great Britain in 2026 by
Carcanet
Main Library, The University of Manchester
Oxford Road, Manchester, M13 9PP
www.carcanet.co.uk

A CIP catalogue record for this book is
available from the British Library.

ISBN 978 1 80017 546 4

Book design by Andrew Latimer, Carcanet
Typesetting by LiteBook Prepress Services
Printed in Great Britain by SRP Ltd, Exeter, Devon

FSC www.fsc.org MIX Paper | Supporting responsible forestry FSC® C014540

The publisher acknowledges financial
assistance from Arts Council England.

Arts Council England
Supported using public funding by
ARTS COUNCIL
ENGLAND

CONTENTS

Desire lines 9
The ragged wing edges of The Comma 10
The very first want 11
Construction Site Futurism 12
How bristles become sketchable 13
How to get out of a pool 14
The Photographer's Organ 15
Angle bracket 16
Is a room without its objects still a room? 17
Can we call a souvenir a heritage? 18
The origins of Say Uncle! 19
INscription 20
Meteorology for outside people 21
De Profundis Babysitter's Club 22
Source material 23
Marriage of Convenience 24
Universal appeal 25
Rage is an outside that wants you back in 26
to be content with almost-fatherlessness 27
Object permanence 28
Car boot sale 30
learning to crow 31
Lovers I have considered loving 32
Generation 33
Heritage sector 34
Communal 35
Table Talk 36
Metasequoia 37
Pegs 38
Meteorology for the blundered 40
Fast Car 41

Since the collective noun for jellyfish is a smack 42
Fortification 43
The untapped potential of water 44
∫ 45
For my brother whom I'm told is getting very tall 47
resisting foregrounding 48
Meteorology for Inside People 50
Coping with other people's expertise: 51
O 52
Why planting trees won't save us 53
Skin graft 54
Back when i too was an egg 55
Just a Little Off 56
The moment before the breaking up when
I want to know how to find the true north of
your middle parting 58
Butch 4 butch 59
Stained Glass 60
Meteorology for the scaffolding 61
Found meteorology 62
Graft 63
Foregrounding 64
How much of the mountain are we bringing back home? 65
Joker 66
Butch Baby Bell 67
Ode to shorts 68
Trying the natural way 69
The collective noun for myths is a foundling 70
The family way 72

Acknowledgements 75

THE NATURAL WAY

DESIRE LINES

Tell me/
When did you first
feel/know you wanted
to do this?

Crow's flight – like a terracotta fillet on the roof nudging its way down, how dogs do, looking for your best smells – yes that's how it was. A village with a name like a tyre crackling over a fallen branch. Places hold onto us like sticky weed. We are not playing chess in a doorway, our socks tacking the nails –

Tell me /
What did you make first?

First, I made arrangements for the doll house, the collapse of its impossible rooms. Like anyone with a name like tomboy, my first love was miniature catastrophes.

Tell me /
When did you know you
were good?

Sunday opens like a nectarine, fissures where the worms have been; maps are carving devices but what happens is more like furrowing. The year I held trowel, trout, boot of abandoned bumper car, doubt like a just -birthed foal, amniotic echoing slick; holding the compass we were born with like a sunned butterfly.

THE RAGGED WING EDGES OF THE COMMA

The butterfly said 'if I could turn back,
unwing myself like jewellery unloosed on the perch of bed
with lips where once the silver could latch infinity,

and take on again many-legged fate,
knowing there's another turn, to feel the almost
of a noduled shoulder stemmed from protruding youth,

I would forfeit that chequered fragility,
that spread of airborne, heady iris and gossamer.
What does the butterfly turn into?

A shrine where all memory of youth
is lost in chrysalis? and that form I once longed
to become, cork-lined, pinned like a brooch.'

THE VERY FIRST WANT

Call me
Foundler. Never
let me finish
my story. Tell
me there's
something foal
in the way I sit
on ferries. It's
just a figure
of speech.

CONSTRUCTION SITE FUTURISM

Begin with scaffold, no scaffolds,
house with scaffold in, with a house
in which scaffolds are *in* with the house it's on,
yes – scaffolding.

Where we were housed, places lean
inside themselves like people do – is it
too much to squat into the temporary
swill – *a place*

to last, spit it out, rinse the sink, let out
a minty *ahh.* We laboured like photographs
with chicken wallpaper, avocado bathrooms.
Imagine owning

enough to make bad design choices. We'll try
for gingerbread, it'll rise thick like I slice toast,
it's better for holding a fort, but does not taste
good, lay out

the pieces, speckle icing with turmeric, coffee,
beetroot, give up on sweetness in aid of colour,
wait for the call. No matter we can eat. No matter
not all waste

is equal, decay will come, we will be in awe
of mushrooms again. I've got a game for you
take a toothpick: who can get the most out
of the crevices.

Later, our shit was a shocking fuchsia.

HOW BRISTLES BECOME SKETCHABLE

Something unfocuses and refocuses.
We have paint in our hair, don't we?
From helping the decorator shuffle
the wardrobe back in place.

Our self-portraiture: meticulously
reattaching all the hair we were born with
and then, the way a sculpture would,
chiselling something impenetrable

into texture, beads under clay,
coins in the cake batter, follicles
swirling in the darkness like salt
in water, taste unfurling with madness.

I can French-braid while walking
only I don't have my own head for it
anymore, but men's eyes move like carbon
and clay buffeting around a drum,

drawing their own moustaches darker,
with their girlfriend's eyebrow pencils.

Something unfocuses and refocuses,
like a question mark does, wet as paint.

HOW TO GET OUT OF A POOL

	Noseclip	Sculling	Synchronised swimming
What does working mean?	Spittle ribbing the inside of your mouth	Pistol - not strong just good machinery	Genius is when you can't keep up with yourself
What does failing mean?	Bubbles are dogged, forget alliance	Death is a bad way of saying you're tired	A birth of a nuisance of octopuses
What are you thinking about?	Not counting	When stunt becomes a verb it means what holds you back	Babies learning to swim before they can walk

THE PHOTOGRAPHER'S ORGAN

Back when I had to wait another hundred years to live, I believed in the end of time, how an ocean ridge believes in a cresting air, how a scurry in the chest believes in feet enough to carry the blood there, how a needle submits to entering, how oil believes itself separate from water, how the photographer believes in stills, how you ask my name because you believe in knowing, how a pipe believes in being filled, how a woodpecker believes in the worthwhile, how an hourglass believes in cartwheels, how this is not what they meant when they gave me a memorable naming, how your last years were a series of split ends, how future believes in the trunk more than the roots, the branch more than the trunk, the bud more than the branch, the seed more than the bud, the sun more than anything. Back when I had waited one hundred years to live, I loved the future like how a belief believes there are no synonyms, how words believe they are worth becoming, how I believes in missing articles, how time is the photographer's organ that must believe in the body before it can be put to work, like how the end of time is at the beginning of things.

ANGLE BRACKET

Halfway down the loop it was not as dark
as we had planned,
with that yard-long box of chorizo, slowing deteriorating
under expected rain.
I offered to hold it while you chose a garden to throw
a bike-light into,

you can hold the same thing
like a baby or like a gun
and it will feel different

after a midnighter in front of the fire
trying to wrench
the angle bracket off the floor so fewer
toes were stubbed,
the ratty silk shirt, and the house
with three pianos
and only sofa cushions. It was nice to meet
someone today
after so many days of having people almost
disappear, to watch
you wind your glass with masking tape
for nothing,
except to busy yourself, grapefruit hair like a
Tudor prince,
letting me carry your inside joke

unboxed and lain across
the red-lined centre of the road – like their
hospital-rash arms.

Let's try it at a different angle, hold it
like a falling slate.

IS A ROOM WITHOUT ITS OBJECTS STILL A ROOM?

Having waited for habitat longer than a person
who believes in the word should it is easy to become
                                                            impatient with pondlife.

Gather the fridges of growth and scull like memories
do, hoping to be retired into souvenirs.

Locks are for people who believe in both *in*
and loss, but a tadpole wellies itself through time,
                                                            like all good commas do.

Before you can ask what a room is you need to know
why a house might want to be more than one thing,

why a place might begin to want privacy, why all
things must be taught the meaning of the word
                                                            consequence.

CAN WE CALL A SOUVENIR A HERITAGE?

'Colette opened Truman's twenty-three-year-old hand. In it she placed a crystal paperweight with a white rose at its centre. "What does it remind you of?" she asked; "What images occur to you?" Truman turned it around in his hand. "Young girls in their communion dresses," he said. The remark pleased Colette. "Very charming," she said. "Very apt. Now I can see what Jean told me is true. He said 'Don't be fooled, my dear. He looked like a ten-year-old angel. But he's ageless and has a very wicked mind.'" She gave it to him as a souvenir.

In theory, any old meteorite could do it, any survivor
of atmosphere heavy enough to anchor those
flutterings; but the archivists gather puddlings
to corral enough Millefiori, and avoid any other
such name, the handing down of an
  unnameable inheritance. In the dense
containment, a bulb which at the right angle
          might set alight your papers, might outsurvive
your thoughts. I never understood trinkets
          until the promise of a souvenir opened my
hand like a flower in anthesis. Oscar Wilde collected
these domes until he died. His tomb was vandalised
by a fabled cemetery manager who souvenired
the testicles into paperweights for his desk.
Very charming   *very apt*
since then, a kiss-   barrier has been
erected around him, as the lipstick grease slowly
took apart the stone. What is glass but a barrier
to everything but light?

THE ORIGINS OF SAY UNCLE!

The parrot is learning sounds not names.
idiom is a very juvenile form of confession.
confession is an ugly way of making
shame into a doing word.

UNCLE

In reception I lied and said I was born
in our Ford Fiesta on the M4,
A boy who had a broken arm but I think
he lied about how it broke.

UNCLE

We once spent an afternoon drawing
a to-scale map of Reading on my patio,
he is still my barometer
for intelligence.

UNCLE

The parrot learning sounds is still saying
meanings it can understand.

UNCLE

I think I told my friend we went on a date
but we just did IQ tests on his home computer.

UNCLE

INSCRIPTION

under the Maiwand Lion
memorial in unmoving
iron, throat ossified
in unending roar; you told
me how the sculptor
threw himself on the
tracks: 'because he did
the legs wrong'.
'her natural posture!'

we exclaimed still in
theatre garb. I played the
young prince, whose
death was too early to
justify my presence so I
joined you in the chorus
where we made up the
starboard and the hull of
Antigonus's ship.

I never told you how
often I got off the bus
early to walk home
with Leontes pretending
admired the unglazing
of her eyes when Hermione
stepped out of the sculpting
of herself – that too-warm
art. I simply agreed

that the sculpture's shame
was justified, that
if I had
to witness those forking
flanks and the youths
daring each other to piss
up the plinth, then I too
might reconsider
my exit,

but we were just sixteen
and only halfway brave,
all our days were the same
awkward length so
we'd never admit the best
parts of the show were

when our masks were on
and we could look 'what a fool
honesty is, and trust!' In
these bottle-green tights,
we all have
the wrong legs.

No one wants to be a mirror, but I'm not opposed to transformation, when glass is formed it is made object by recurrence, by turning up in man-made places, by becoming craft. Glass is a state of matter not a single material, glass forms when the molten thing cools so quickly crystalline structures can't reform, they have no time to rearrange themselves. It is a loss of the privilege of memory, a body that has been denied time. Glass is the visible trauma of weather on matter, and I have always found sense and calm in imagining my body as somehow glass-spongelike, my skeleton is petrified into an out-of-timeness, stillness, holding no memory of what changes around it. I have always wanted to undo myself from hourglass, to petrify time, to refuse reconstruction, to imagine myself both as volcano and the matter being denied reformation. Loving could become a series of interrupting recurrences, the smoothness of glass, the undoing of lattice shape. The way a nettle stings you is by syringes of minuscule glass needles, the same material as when the glass in a frame breaks and you bleed onto a photograph. I understand the impermanence of work upon the body. I understand the desire – for resolution, for meeting the structures through which your grief was struck. And of course, I worry you will not change when I change, I worry you are not changing when I am changing, I worry that when we reform you will not love glass. But I choose glass not sand, I choose the stormy hot of annealers, brushing up the broken glass as part of the ritual-work, it will be used again

DE PROFUNDIS BABYSITTER'S CLUB

When I had the same years as a year has months,
Romeo and Juliet ran in the Abbey Ruins opposite
the DFS. Juliet was my babysitter. When Paris died,
he breathed so much I got scared of over-life.
On the prison wall, a giant spider distsracted
from the ruins. Prince began, and the alarm shook
the capsule of blood out of Juliet's pocket.

When I say spider, I mean I didn't expect
a man's body, I mean the wailing
alarm felt like part of the production,
I mean I was distracted by the body
of the girl who taught me how to write
backwards. A prison is a building where

the inside matters most, like a balloon. A ruin
is where we put all the absences. When they
closed the Gaol, celebrities flocked to read
De Profundis, to tour the only cell they thought
a poet might have been: they saved Reading from
an artless future. I'm telling you this from the inside

of my neighbour's downstairs toilet.
No one told me the lock was broken.
There is a six year old who wants to know
when his mum is coming home. Hometown
is a word trying to make itself special; we grow
into cities like coats, like boxes with first shoes.

SOURCE MATERIAL

Sunday: our bodies thirteened in
the shadow of the coach
a man in the trees glugging
an eight-pinter of milk, with eyes
that followed like a painting,
and a hand missing beneath
his zipper like a magic
trick. We scaled
boiled eggs together, I was so careful.

MARRIAGE OF CONVENIENCE

This oily summit of August, the brilliance
of crickets, drying off your arms
like insect do, the dress we both fit in,
pleats. When I say seeking, you say
finding somewhere to walk towards,
around a rockface trilling with air –

motion sickness

we were spoused in a dinghy where the rushes
grow, hay hemmed together into a galleon
of youth – me: a plaque to wanderlust – you:
mole-ish ode to undergrowth, romanced
by the tugging of a worm. Read me again –

lavender motion
                                        sickness

this is the kind of place where people describe wind,
how it tastes limbic – I don't suppose you thought
to bring? No. Old ovals where your glasses
pressed against your face. Elbowless dresses,
a certain way of sitting, a handkerchief tied in
corners around your scalp, the opposite of a glance,
the forecast was unseasonably foggy. Am I telling it right?

UNIVERSAL APPEAL

When I was an illusionist, my mother held me
to the light like a bank note to check
I was real, and I was, even when I was sincerely blank.

I was always more afraid of being left
alone on earth than leaving it. The universe is not in
the accident of a bee sting on

your pinky finger, it's not in the space under the oven where the hamster
once escaped – it did not understand drama,
only how to disappear. There is nothing like knowing

things you made no pact with cannot betray you
- hold out your hand to grasp the light, spit in it if you like,
the universe is in the white fizz.

RAGE IS AN OUTSIDE THAT WANTS YOU BACK IN

want is a word you don't always have
make nurse a verb
make patient a badge that you can remove
the pink off

smarting? You should know
better is a neighbour who still
has a milkman
'when you are better' is
the opposite of time
time is the neighbour who
won't mend the fence
because it is your fence
a fence is a neighbour
who won't learn your name
you don't need a name
until you can want
this very bad idea
is keeping you alive
alive is a feeling
that you cannot hide

TO BE CONTENT WITH ALMOST-FATHERLESSNESS

and a future without
making a father of anyone –
no sharp or flat,
nor natural –

he was an accident
and I was a different kind of accidental
(unfurling) like a myth
or a fuchsia.

OBJECT PERMANENCE

All better now?

Plea small   as webbed foot
glue peeled from hand like chicken sinew
skin dry as   pencil shavings
baby eczema runs   in us like your nose
but halfing surely is the best way to know
               where smells are coming from
like avocado *baby*   plump
as watermelon   talcum pat – pat
(don't breathe in!   all better now?   *baby!*)

                              I must go, children will need goodbyes
so, call this day trip   waving in the train
you are flat   with your legs whirring   like bargemen on pub signs
     like when you learnt   your socks can come off   wiggle wiggle
wee wee wee

                                        I can see you there!

All better now?   Your mother was an antenna
  that fuzzed all night
I don't like to ask questions   who kept who awake
     Shunting tracks and hauling freight
It is better you never knew   me: 'sister'
only ceramic face   somewhere in
the wedding video   continental plates
drift as fast   as fingernails grow

all better now?

they're the really useful crew

Why do little boys love to wave in trains?

Be they diesel be they steam
And no one can remember when
there didn't used to be words

All better now?   there's this place in the indent of my scalp
where the ventouse hoovered me right out   that patch of dry skin
lingers   sometimes when I am on a train with its lungs inverted,
I have an ugly fantasy

That I got it from you
You beautiful briny *baby*

CAR BOOT SALE

Believe in suspension,
without thinking of bridges

or the time a babysitter
flew you off the road,

up, I mean, on the way
to a car boot sale,

where a little boy desperate
for your LEGO castle

came minutely to fill
his pocket with what he could

grasp, hoping to build or at least
wiggle with delight

all the way home knowing
one castle had a window

it didn't before.

LEARNING TO CROW

the unbuttoned eight of us, crowding into
the small behind a curtain, triple-mirrored,
comparing cup sizes. Of the collective,
I was the largest, bulked up early.
None of us had the kind of pyjamas
people wore to bed, only stocking fillers, dinosaurs,
Glitter Babe and I Need My Beauty
Sleep – we saw them in life-saving classes.
They clung to us worse than skimpy cozzies, the year
someone told me bellies protrude
only until your chest grew bigger,
the way roosters do –
stupor resounding across the acres
of morning or on
until it.

LOVERS I HAVE CONSIDERED LOVING

In the enclave of pelican's mouth I have slept, quietly ungenerous
with the parts of me that generate respect, a paramour for haruspex:
I have undulated with the swallowings this bird regrets, I have girdled
the world and back for just one breath, I have closeted in the tremor
of its neck, I have sanctioned every fish it ever met, I have been prostrate
and repressed, I have salted myself into rejuvenation and I have rutted for
the rest. Isn't that the work of all good plumbing? A dyke provides
land with a wall; embankment to prevent flooding.

GENERATION

Do you remember the story of the hailstone the size of a lightbulb,
how the windscreen calved like an iceberg?

What do you believe in
when you compress your face into ice?
Feel your eyeballs crystalise,
can you see
the future: a menopausal woman zipping and unzipping my jacket.
Like I used to strip and redress my dolls;

Here, a trunk of land on a conveyer belt,
A grotto in a wave – Johnson's No More Tears –

hoping to see something different?

I remember the story
I've heard it before.
Believing isn't the problem.
I hate to think about the probability
we will end like 'eureka!' began,
buoying gold in bathwater to measure its worth,

something between the triumph of discovery
and the shame of being discovered.

HERITAGE SECTOR

If you call piers and bridges cousins
you understand the legacy of water,

our grandparents holding up tiles
their fathers made, the letters with
old names on them, grand as weighted

curtains. This is nothing, right?
A shore freezing out to the place where it can't,
a bucket of crabs, a gorgeous hemtide of kelp,

like bobbles on a jumper.

COMMUNAL

May I, speak for us, I mean?

The five valleys calling to the sky,
the way we once did, too far
from home and all of us desperate

to piss. In the full common of snow,
bizarrely lit for midnight, like a white
sofa in a house full of dogs;

and each of us, bare as peeled potatoes,
burning holes in the snow - it almost would have been worth

it to be seen.

TABLE TALK

+ + + + + + + + + + + + + +
+ +++++++ + +++++++ + +++++++ + +++++++ +
+ table + inch + comment + pinch +
+ cloth + burn + tator + totem +
+ ____ + ____ + ____ + ____ +
* the stars * for special * silver * place *
* come out * occasions * hardy * mats *
+ * be * longing * yourself * in
spectacle me imagining edges
+ begging + invisi- + by hud- + into +
+ for + bility * dling + something +
+ ____ +
+ I can + where + tasked + making +
+ call home + you are + with + it +
small cardboard boxed
+ + + + * + * + + * + + *
* you too * way our + whimsy- + symbols *
* like the * mother's + stars + of *
+ ____ + ____ + ____ + ____ +
* occas * as a kind * allow- * unanswered *
* ions * of stopping * ing for * asterisk *
+ +++++++ + +++++++ + +++++++ + +++++++ +
+ + + + + + + + + + + + + +

*When in the woods, our largeness made us titled as tablecloth, picking out the stars from the mud, their silver ugly celebration, flecks of presence that is not ours, count them into a sum of asterisks, answers out of time with their moment.

METASEQUOIA

I am selfish enough to follow you into the brush,
that musky common where orchids bud from Amberley mounds,
and the canal, now groaning, dry with old ploughs
and lingonberry, where we turned back before we could reach
the source - the Thames Head. How did you find me,
even here where I have bolted to recover
the keys in the last dwindling, between the great calf-heavy
bodies of cows settling in for the dew? You will have to
come back each November, to watch the saplings
progress. Somewhere my scatterings,
there is a dawn Redwood stunned by its ardent
belief that it has to grow, and its equal shame that it must.

PEGS

How ashamed you'd be
of how little I work, how unbruised
my mind is by the scaffolding
of occupation, how neatly dusted.

Your husband still posts me
articles about our great – great – greats
who ran bus companies in Australia,
and history is important but

it's easy to compare a mind
to a house, to the thatch roof
on your first home together,
and you leading the engine

through every village, stomach
round as onion, as orange,
as another brain. It is easy to
compare the secretarying

of these moments, shorthand
but somehow not believing
in memory enough
to leave it undocumented.

What did they mean when they said
you were comfortable?
Was it the memory-lossing itself:
The warehouse becoming a theatre,

the old mill becoming a studio,
the churches becoming blocks of flats,
the typewriters becoming display pieces,
the secretaries becoming computers,

the grandchildren becoming artists?
How do I make your name more
than a figure of speech, more than
an octothorpe named for its interruption?

I want to build something,
but I don't think it should be a place,
it should be more than memory
memorising itself on the page.

A secretarying of the moment,
an octothorpe, named for its interruption,
the kind of article my grandchildren
will find difficult to read,   because they too have a future.

METEOROLOGY FOR THE BLUNDERED

future I made in your wake
hurried like toads
when rain falls, ceremonial,
I take no umbrage
only that to remember you
properly is to
remember myself and to
remember myself
is to unsolidify. They put
guardrails up
on ships because they know
we love edges
can never contain ourselves

to the centre
but to visit again, now I am
beginning something
new, something furrowless,
smooth as the sun
eddying into undergrowth,
ships into the night
must still signal to each other
the swinging of
revelation as he bows his cap
and calls out to the wild darkness
I am recovering
from the future already.

FAST CAR

Standing in the stack
of car magazines in the garage,
you could never feel
the rush of a long and empty
dual carriageway, flooring it
until our lungs cladded
into the leather, trying to recreate
that Vanquish in Motion ad:

a scene subtitled *closed*
track professional drivers.
Cruising feels too dangerous,
Let's try for 90. My urge to sing
over the revving *somebody's got to*:
I have never loved a car.

Except to scuttle like a loose
bolt into your engine,
stunted between pistons,
muddled into stroke
and spark, confused into revolution:
be someone be someone
be someone.

SINCE THE COLLECTIVE NOUN FOR JELLYFISH IS A SMACK

unscrapped blue   tentacled thread   embroidered jellyfish
squat yellow
spy-like taste   sunwet nivea   beached jellyfish
safe imaginings
unclenched beach   translucent afternoon   stimed photographs
splitting things

Jellyfish is the common
Name for the Medusa
Phase of certain
Members of
The Subphylum Medusozoa

free-swimming bell   trailing anchor   bodysoft pulse
doesn't it just smack of given name?

FORTIFICATION

In the tunnelling outside Madjeski's house,
with the concrete smooth and high –
I don't want to use the word impenetrable –
the cameras are figureheads.
At a certain height you can see the foxes.

I am wearing your thick curmudgeonly socks
and windbreaker with the meshy pockets
and cinema tickets, because I never bring the right
clothing. You are proud of your dog,
his eccentric symmetry to you.

He does not need a lead because his last owner
was the right kind of angry, and he's only broken
your trust once, to rummage in a dead fish.
How like thieves we feel trellising along the public
paths by anxious houses. Maybe you named

me for my keeping up with things, from the top
of the plateau, first the tilling fields, then the wisps of
the largest town, like baby hairs.

THE UNTAPPED POTENTIAL OF WATER

When teaching is an impossible thing
some liquids fold like   tulle,
tidal,   (barricade or barracuda)
                  how the years have been   tidal
foolish:
                  kind as spelling out:

S K I N   G R A F T

The water will not   stop moving!

In the birthing pool   there is a moment between foetus   and baby
where we are almost gilled,   when the body falls
                  open,   when these liquids   fold together:
meringue or merengue;   how the years have been
                  and you have been   watered
gulp and tonsil   bulb and tourniquet

when teaching is the impossible thing
know that water cannot follow   you back up the waterpipe

∫

For Sister talk
+define yourself first? Narrow those words into predefined definitions. I mean narrow like burrowing into the small intricates
like nanoscientists do

In spite don't be spiteful
of some great divide where does your equation begin? Is this one equation?
I am knowing state your knowledge system
you not as descendant
but ladder-upright later you say this
was a feather but
they fall horizontally

+ Plummeting don't feathers drift?
as feathers do
convinced the wing
has plenty
to go on
+symbol = symbolism you content
to journey with
not against
the uncanny sky
+ some feathered
impressionism
laddered for
resistance
+ imagining yourself
< clear as rain
you must define what is included in < to use ∈ here you must
define what the limitations of the rain are (time/ distance/space) if/then rain is less rigorously defined

rain ⇒plumage

+ sticking the
landing
> blasting
+ frankness
∈ friendship
as integral
or rather
>

No that's not what integral in maths means. Nothing needs to be integrated in mathematics, there is no need for maths, it just describes the world and what will happen anyway. Stop trying to intervene.

FOR MY BROTHER WHOM I'M TOLD IS GETTING VERY TALL

I can only recall the terrific
bronze squeamish of your foot sole,
you, unseasoned,
still heavied by your origins.

You were such a good fighter,
bucking at the belt of yourself.

You could be empty *and* whole,
like an Athenian vase,
but when your heirloom is diving,
not every sport should leave no entry mark.

This is an unlearnt wish,
like blowing out your brother's candle,
but stay long enough to scorch,
for me to call 'heel!'
to find your prints in the clay like a wax seal,

for you to become ordinary,
you wriggling bale of legend,
you flammable lunging myth.

RESISTING FOREGROUNDING

All the other uncles were terrible
at mouthing   *Retreat Retreat*   but your position
is how I remember where the goal is.
Mouthguard fallen through   *EN GARDE*   hockey puckering the pitch.
                                                    Retreat Retreat

You were on my sidelines mouthing
foul as anything, the old maps of pitches trailing like leads,
me dribbling like an old dog into penalty:

                                                                What did she call you?
                                                    Retreat Retreat

mouth again: try grounding the ball   try matching others   try lining up
   the compass

land hikes up its skirt, the question
of orientation in kingless chess,
knowing as you did
(mouth it at me like breakfast food)   /knowing as others did
geography trailing as you did/ trailed as you were
                                                    Retreat Retreat

still fleecing like a badluck holiday; all of us huddled
on the beach still hockeying the sand.

Unscored like your putdown dog, or unprepared soil, or unrisen bread –

/ puttering down /*what did she call you* / puttering out / *was it what she*
   called me

A person isn't a side, right? I can't hold onto mouthing
from the sidelines, it's not enough. I can't orient
myself to goal with you standing there waiting for a match.
If you had not made yourself a compass, had not made
me ask for your definitions of the word *retreat*.

METEOROLOGY FOR INSIDE PEOPLE

You have learnt to read with the knowledge that each
lightning strike holds the potential
for fulgurites, and glass

keeps becoming without you and
I am working with the cumulus
to source that

misplaced reputation, blubbering
the way spittled oil thanks
water for its platitudes.

Weather appears
the way scabs remind you
of falling,

undiscovered peaks rarely have relief
maps, and although never
is a place,

recovery is a kind of evaporating.

COPING WITH OTHER PEOPLE'S EXPERTISE:

Not Digging not after Seamus Heaney

Raking out of alliance to the dirt,
the disaster comes then begins to twine
into frame, something like growth
muscles amongst the stubs
of worms, a trowel still warm
from cleaving, you have tried to prune
water, rummaged in the clear, sores
stalking up into miniatures: believe me,
I never thought I could be comfortable
collaborating with weather –

but I hoped I could find a place inside
where the urge to plunge your fingers in the butter
surpassed the world. Perhaps the perfect diver
never quite sees the crowd, only a quiet
most would not allow themselves

to imagine. Once I have learnt the word
sincerity I do not name the teacher. Why does beauty
feel like a risk? Start finishing
the one you're on,   dig.

o

Is it odd to say your lover reminds you of a tree?
Is it odd to say you have a lover, can you have a thing that grows?
I admit I have wanted, even asked, for cruelty from a root tantrumming out of the pavement,
It is true there is a sycamore doubled over in my radiator, humming with consent,
shedding coat hangers; it is true you can make legends of living things.
It is true, many times, on little dark nights I have muttered into the canopy
Spruce up, yes, it's true, I have renamed my skin bark for you.

WHY PLANTING TREES WON'T SAVE US

I cannot solve the unjust livery of
headlines but I will not simplify them
into a reenactment of leaves,

nor imagine the commotion of bodies
trussed in bark, like history is a weekend
past-time where the most expensive

costume wins. I will not make trees
stand in for politics, as if they have
no bodies of their own. I will not

sit in a National Trust Garden,
noting the shoulders of trail trees
and calling myself helpless to nature.

SKIN GRAFT

The day I succeeded in forgetting you exist
my mother rang to call me a grafter again,
I cannot picture my own hands like usual,
I cannot frame the woodpile, those once-
were trees with their age exposed, I
cannot bear the memory of lifting
them into the wheelbarrow, and then of course
later into our fire. How do you time the world
by when a new log is required, transporting
the heat to another part of the tree? I wonder,
handless, if I can be without knowing somewhere
you are burning, but I can, I think I can.

BACK WHEN I TOO WAS AN EGG

under a red light, held in by the burden
of proof, a fissure felt like forever.
How can the shelled chick know
what it is breaking into?
A fist opening for the first time
believes fingers are flags
waving into meaning.

JUST A LITTLE OFF

There is no language
to describe the right haircut,
trim? no, no, there, no

closein, more leftish, rightial,
uppity, no upso, uplier.
dubious. Curliage like foliage,

un-be-bush, brush?
Can you translate what I'm
trying… the last person,

see? like the picture,
no no, gesture – picture,
a pitcher of someone else,

but call it only likeness,
like this, that's a bad angle,
in my gesture it is only

possibility, promise,
half - no not half-hearted,
I am trying. Parting?

The middle is fine,
I know it grows back,
but I can't even interpret

my own body. No, a hat?
I don't suit. What do I want?
The same, the same as

usual, which of course
in haircutting terms
translates to

back the way it was.
To you, my stranger
it means only to

estimate my growth
patterns. How long?
How long like this?

How long? Like this.

THE MOMENT BEFORE THE BREAKING UP WHEN I WANT TO KNOW HOW TO FIND THE TRUE NORTH OF YOUR MIDDLE PARTING

Thinking in oranges, oiled and slick   just before you bury the sun in the suds,   those tubular flowers that coil like   minnows resisting the combmouth   of rakes that claim the stature of whales,   paving stones like ferries, arrows roiling   in the mouth like fiddlesticks,   I have often thought to call you: wicker men and wiccan women,   blinking bricks like thinking children,   cribs and cribbage, fibs and fibula;   singular webbed face - the ritual   of fiction, a west-facing garden, a spider   for iris, leaf of papyrus, a pardon   like chucked chin, a lido inside   a limousine, a limoncello movie scene,   god I miss your runner beans, your hardly   ever, your orange-thinker, slick divides,   divining the oily foibles of my scalp,   burying the lead so terrier-bulbs can   scrimmage out, I almost finished the ruse it is   true, I would rename my skin bark   for you, in a moment we'll agree, growing   is the right thing to do.

BUTCH 4 BUTCH

Visibly Venus, this violence between us is angular, angling out.
Inside is feeling the absence of doubt, doughboy,
reclaiming the face of fed up of this mouth.
Despite my best efforts, masculine
comprehensibility is like refilling
the grout. In this old angle of up,
I'm just looking out for you –
when something's held
together properly,
you aren't supposed to feel the glue.

STAINED GLASS

(For my future-queers)

Today I'll do the glass cutting
to cover where the weather gets in,
phthalo blue and quinac rust,
swap out heat for sharpness,
dip cutter into turpentine and score –
wheelbarrow of curves, grooves,
cures coming apart, colours like a map
much better than brick, or light.

The problem comes about the frame,
I stretch the lead, putty and glaze,
just right for the break in. It makes
good on its measuring promise,
a face wavering in a leaf of light.
The thing about the chrysalis, what
happens within, is that the body melts
and reforms except these tiny

imaginal disks there in the body
from the moment of beginning, wings,
antennae, and the parts of the brain
that retain memory, like furniture
losing its colour in brightness. I want
to see your blue and rust, the places
where colour needs no adjective, least
of all stained, where light begins to swim.

METEOROLOGY FOR THE SCAFFOLDING

'Hallelujah,' says the igloo
to the snow, 'I can call
myself not!' A brick-
layer can bear the present,
how it clatters into focus,
is recreated above ground.

FOUND METEOROLOGY

As a pinecone falls apart
windowsill-dry with the mystery
of insideness. You did not have
to pick it – but plants show love by asking

you to take them apart, undo their fruit,
migrate, swill, remake them. Isn't that
what it feels like? Like you were never
meant to be one thing.

Your pinecone looks like a knuckle holding a tooth,
or a cave that doesn't believe empty

is a word at all, and wants the word *around*
to be held. I love all your dying parts,
I shall not call you inspiration,
here has no business being defined by its origin.

GRAFT

You said you had no patience for people who say, 'I'd love to do that,'
but never do. My favourite photograph is the bungalow-gutting.
What can you teach me about productive destruction? You, the kind
of person who will let a house be knocked down and feel no urge
to break a window. Let me pour a slab, lay a drain, read the spirit level.

But there - in the photographs of rebuild the mesh of retaining walls,
orange tarpaulin, a fortnight of muck, the rubble like tilled soil,
scaly pre-torrential sand, rink of sluiced concrete: admit your courage,
for once, without asking where it is coming from.

FOREGROUNDING

Holding
    down the lift button
        with the finger still plucky
    with your scent don't you think
            it's hot
that I've no time for
    my potential anymore

    I've been fucking strategy
    documents   they're always
wet for me

    last night I dreamt
my boss drove me
    to a laser quest we agreed
    there was nothing inherently
    misogynistic about masculinity

    she held the wheel
        between   her knees
and I formatted a thought
            just for myself

halfway   through   stapling
        it's the hardest thing
            I've ever done
        I've got a retractable badge holder now
        like the hot girls
        at school

HOW MUCH OF THE MOUNTAIN ARE WE BRINGING BACK HOME?

And we were thinking less of beauty and more of risks
– those gorgeous ones when you can slip out of a shirt

like water out of a glass. I was further behind,
hiking in denim towards the craggy

promise of falling, or a grotto pebbled into its own pocket
where we might find some underwear behind a rock,

like another dock leaf, and to think of you – there – held up
in the water by me buoying you into shore… See how long you

can hold your breath, and yourself, open to the cool difference,
yes, fucking in nature because it looks like us

not like men in poems.
Don't you know the countryside code: take everything with you.

JOKER

Amniotic fluid does not scan
well, it blinks, nurtures
a lying downwards – magnifying
glass of pestle –
future mortal,
future knock knock.

BUTCH BABY BELL

I didn't think you'd want to hear
how we made a place for you –

born hipbearless
blunt envelope of arm
brick bulkied –

how we couldn't fit you inside
some lost red sea.

Surely, it's all just a birth metaphor,
how we built a city inside of ourselves,

yes foundling, yes founding, yes fond,
of course, fondness.

That's not the way they would say it,
no one thinks of a city before a house.

How many fishbowls did we march inside the aqueduct with?
Inventory mulling out before us,

like bulbs, or fields, or machinery.

ODE TO SHORTS

so short our boxers tease out underneath
that square of thigh, airing itself –
the afterwork special – good for tethering and walking into water.

The way our knees almost touched across the room, across our generations,
across words you have had longer with;

the perfect arrogance of a tan line,
just enough space for a hand to reach all the way to our hips,
or to test our lunges against a fissure of earth.

Won't you see me properly for once?
My morning unzipping of the tent
to crouch in the earth
shorts suspended

and piss.

God, I want to be me.

TRYING THE NATURAL WAY

The night we decide to become
snail parents, you make an anthropology
video about them for class, about the nature
of care and moving in – the way people like us
do. One morning we wake to the escapologist
stuck firmly to our door, and later a grandmother
introduces two babies in the park. We decide
to start with the natural way.

There can be nothing accidental in our making,
despite your insistence that I remove you from
the birthing pool if you vomit,
or the ever-long list of names like the tendrils
on our bathroom fern. These are secure, we
are simply fermenting together, pressing
down the cabbage leaves. In many ways
we can make nothing but a future,

except of course, we are always finding new
trailing ancient beings to name.

THE COLLECTIVE NOUN FOR MYTHS IS A FOUNDLING

This ending is connective tissue. This ending is a freak show. This ending is psychosomatic. This ending is a cold case. This ending does not define you. This ending is a shibboleth. This ending is a symbol. Don't be scared, you get to say what it means. This ending is easy: you love your mother, you are loved by women, miraculously without precedent. Things happen that you don't have a name for. Snow keeps making angels every year. This ending is low resolution: teaching is an impossible thing, but the camera moves through scenes like water. This ending is the history of the world. One person's fury ends a nation. England yells I wish I'd never been born! into the rafters. This ending forgot who its focus was. Big as a word can be, all-necked creature, only remembers the jellyfish, only births the placenta, only believes acrobats when they are walking with fear in their eyes. This ending ends, although I know that is not possible. This ending contains traces of an impossible thing: the water will not stop moving. This ending was written by a child we love who knows she does not know all words. This ending you should not show your mother. We fucked to forget we wanted a daughter. Like all good fucking it forgot what it could make, like all good ends we slept after, like all good love we believed in invention not discovery, now we write in the margins of each other. This ending is married to its work, builds a whole world of statues, blocks out the sun, loves only people in glass houses, sells paperweights to presidents, to bankers, to stacks of paper, to collectors, to collectives, to office climates, gets conjunctivitis, traps ghosts in glass coffins like lepidopterists. When they recover the body, the pontil marks look like a strange disease. This ending is a collective noun. The ending is Jane Doe: we all bury our names in the dirt like eggs for hatching, instead they grow like statues of our bodies, our likenesses scare us. Looking at each other turns us to stone. This ending is source material: we define ourselves first, narrow those words into definition, I mean narrow like burrowing into the intricacies, I mean like mathematicians do. This ending is a revival of the Electra Complex: it is not decent, we double-tongue like oboes do, ducking, bowing, full of bloom. I make myself parental figurine, conquest. This ending has been contaminated with the right not to disclose. It says kidnapping tunnels us a future, says Atlantis was made before it was lost so let's build something we can sink with. This ending will not admit its addictions, its leadless existence, its locomotion, its crop circle forehead, lets us age badly. Bottles are just future disintegration. This ending wants to know if you've tried meditation, medication, consummation, consecration. This ending gets off on this, witnessing, suspecting something like a poltergeist. This ending is survival: like fawns, no like wolves hiding in the nettle, this gulley galleria. A sink/sinkhole is a place where dirt disappears. We inherit something close to too much time, this ending's greatest pride is keeping you alive, although of course you did all the work, our fenderer, our tenderest query, our evergreen hand. They adjust to it don't they, the seasick fishermen? We change the locks, so we have a door like everybody else, I have no proof that endings end anything. I do not want to keep writing in order to prove we exist. This ending is inheritance. This ending is a premonition. This ending is a utopia. This ending is none of your concern. This ending is blue da ba de da ba die. This ending is a non-intrusive translation. This ending is a bad interpretation. This ending is a distraction. This ending is a first aid kit. This ending is an hourglass. This ending is all in your head. This ending is not a bildungsroman, what you feel is coming is coming.

THE FAMILY WAY

How can I possibly answer the question
of beginning, the second coming
harnessing us together? Isn't it bizarre
how euphemism grinds, when you
tell me to marry my inventiveness
with restraint, in Gretna Green,
in a linen suit, in a fickle tense,
in hot pursuit, on a construction site,
in a hard hat, under a lintel, under
a banner, under duress, under milk
wood, under the hood, do you think
we should? Could we fit inside all
the buttons like bullrushes?
Do you think we could,
have I mean?

ACKNOWLEDGEMENTS

Thank you to all the team at Carcanet, John, Michael, Andrew and Jazmine; for the love and respect you've shown my work, especially Andrew for the incredibly challenge of formatting my mad poems. John, who has championed my work, and got deep in the weeds of word choice with me for nearly a decade. Thank you to New Writing North for the Northern Poetry Award that got me over the last hill of this book.

Some of these poems were originally published in other magazines including:

Inscription is part of project *OUTscription* produced in the archives Manchester Metropolitan University's Special Collections and first presented at University of Manchester's Sexuality Summer School. *Metasequoia* was first published in The Interpreter's House.

Just a little off was commissioned by Factory International responding to MIF 2019's show *Studio Creole. Back when I too was an egg* was first published in The North. *Butch4Butch* first appeared as part of my 2022 show *LOB* supported by Contact Theatre and Arts Council England.

To poets and friends who have read and listened generously, and inspired me with their own ideas, especially to Frankie Blaus, Alle Bloom, Shaun Hill, Isaiah Hull, Sarah-Joy Ford, Keisha Thompson, Chris Brown and Kayleigh Jayshree who has seen and reviewed many iterations of this collection.

To my family, Mama and Megs, thank you for teaching me the meaning of passion, work, and love; I choose you every time.

And finally, to Ruth, my bear with mountains inside, without whom this book would have been entirely different, entirely less full of future; thank you for holding the punty with me.